EGYPT'S Ancient Secrets

TOMB ROBBERS

Stolen Treasures

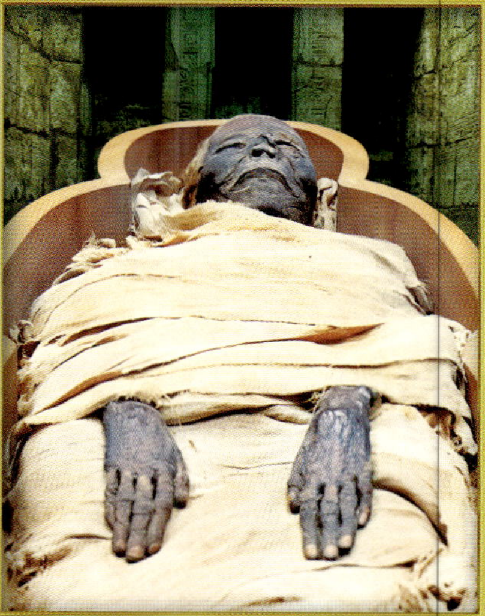

by Ruth Owen

Consultant: Dr. Christopher Naunton
Egyptologist

BEARPORT PUBLISHING

New York, New York

Credits

Cover and Title Page, © Federico Rostagno/Shutterstock; 4, © Danita Delimont/Alamy; 5, © Nerthuz/Shutterstock, © Fedor Selivanov/Shutterstock, © Shipov Oleg/Shutterstock, and © Tereshchenko Dmitry/Shutterstock; 6, © World History Archive/Alamy; 7T, © Heritage Image Partnership/Alamy; 7B, © Federico Rostagno/Shutterstock; 8, © Robert Harding/Alamy; 9L, © Granger Historical Picture Archive/Alamy; 9R, © Alessandro Vannini/Getty Images; 10T, © Christian Jegou Publiphoto Diffusion/Science Photo Library; 10C, Public Domain; 10B, © World History Archive/Alamy; 11T, © Alessandro Vannini/Getty Images; 11B, © Dea/W. Buss/Getty Images; 12TL, © Heritage Image Partnership Ltd/Alamy; 12C, © leomagdala/Shutterstock; 12B, © Avprophoto/Shutterstock; 13, © Werner Forman/Getty Images; 14, Public Domain; 15, © antonbelo/Shutterstock; 16T, Public Domain; 16B, © mspoli/Shutterstock; 17, © srgktk/Shutterstock; 17B, Public Domain; 18–19, © Ruby Tuesday Books; 20–21, © Dorothy Puray-Isidro/Shutterstock; 20B, © Ruby Tuesday Books; 21, © Gary Doak/Alamy; 22, © eFesenko/Shutterstock; 23L, Public Domain; 23BR, Public Domain; 24, © Science Photo Library; 25, © Khaled Desouki/AFP/Getty Images; 26, Public Domain; 27, © epa european pressphoto agency b.v./Alamy; 28, © Getty Images; 29T, © Vladimir Wrangel/Shutterstock; 29B, © Columbia Pictures/Getty Images.

Publisher: Kenn Goin
Editor: Jessica Rudolph
Creative Director: Spencer Brinker
Photo Researcher: Ruby Tuesday Books Ltd

Library of Congress Cataloging-in-Publication Data

Names: Owen, Ruth, 1967– author.
Title: Tomb robbers : stolen treasures / by Ruth Owen.
Other titles: Egypt's ancient secrets.
Description: New York, New York : Bearport Publishing Company, 2017. | Series: Egypt's ancient secrets | Includes bibliographical references and index.
Identifiers: LCCN 2016052699 (print) | LCCN 2016054954 (ebook) | ISBN 9781684020263 (library) | ISBN 9781684020782 (Ebook)
Subjects: LCSH: Tombs—Egypt—Valley of the Kings—Juvenile literature. | Grave robbing—Egypt—Valley of the Kings—Juvenile literature. | Grave goods—Egypt—Valley of the Kings—Juvenile literature. | Egypt—History—To 332 B.C.—Juvenile literature.
Classification: LCC DT73.T6 O94 2017 (print) | LCC DT73.T6 (ebook) | DDC 932—dc23
LC record available at https://lccn.loc.gov/2016052699

For more information, write to Bearport Publishing Company, Inc., 45 West 21st Street, Suite 3B, New York, New York 10010.
Printed in the United States of America.

10 9 8 7 6 5 4 3 2 1

Contents

Searching for a Tomb 4
Robbers! 6
Treasure-Filled Tombs 8
A Mummy for All Time 10
Grave Goods for Sale 12
Who Were the Robbers? 14
The Story of a Thief. 16
The Worst Punishment 18
Stopping the Thieves 20
The Hidden Mummies. 22
Mixed-Up Mummies 24
Then and Now. 26

Egypt's Ancient Secrets 28
Glossary. 30
Bibliography. 31
Read More 31
Learn More Online 31
Index 32
About the Author 32

Searching for a Tomb

It was a hot night in the Egyptian desert more than 3,100 years ago. On the west bank of the Nile River, across from the city of Thebes (THEEBZ), eight men were hard at work. They were using copper tools to dig a tunnel through the stone **tomb** of the ancient Egyptian king **Pharaoh** Sobekemsaf (soh-buh-KEM-suhf). Finally, the rock in front of the men cracked and fell away, leaving a dark hole.

The Valley of the Kings was one place that ancient Egyptians buried their pharaohs.

The desert on the west bank of the Nile River was known as the land of the dead. That's because people saw the sun set, or die, in the west each night. The ancient Egyptians buried their dead in this area.

Trembling with fear and excitement, the men lifted their flaming torches and peered inside the tomb. For more than 450 years, Pharaoh Sobekemsaf's tomb had remained undisturbed. Now its contents were in danger. The men were tomb robbers! They would stop at nothing to steal the beautiful treasures buried with the king.

Robbers!

One of the tomb robbers was a young **stonemason** named Amenpanufer (AH-men-pa-nuh-fur). He and his **accomplices** stepped into the tomb and found two large stone coffins called **sarcophagi**. The men strained to push aside the heavy lid of one sarcophagus. Inside was the pharaoh's incredible wooden coffin, decorated with gold, silver, and jewels. Amenpanufer and the other robbers opened the coffin's lid. The king's **mummy** was inside!

An ancient Egyptian stone sarcophagus

The mummy was covered with more shiny gold and dazzling jewels. The greedy robbers tore at the mummy, pulling off its precious jewelry. Then the thieves opened the other sarcophagus and wooden coffin. Inside was the pharaoh's queen. The thieves stole the jewels from her mummy, too.

The men hurriedly gathered every valuable item they could carry. Then, to cover their tracks, they set fire to the royal coffins and escaped into the night.

On that night, Amenpanufer and the other thieves stole 32 pounds (14.5 kg) of gold from Sobekemsaf's tomb!

A pharaoh might have been buried wearing a solid gold collar like this one.

Treasure-Filled Tombs

The tombs of pharaohs, queens, and other important people were filled with treasures. Why? The ancient Egyptians thought that when a person died, he or she lived on in the **afterlife**. In order to do this, the dead person's **spirit** would need food, clothes, furniture—all the things they had used in life. Wealthy Egyptians were also buried with their **pendants**, gold, and other valuable possessions.

A pendant

The people of ancient Egypt believed their pharaoh was a god who lived on earth. Once a pharaoh died, he would live among other gods in the afterlife. To show his **status** as a god king, a pharaoh would need beautiful clothes, jeweled collars, bracelets, and rings. All these objects, and many others, were placed inside his tomb.

The tomb of Pharaoh Tutankhamen (*too*-tahn-KAH-men), known as King Tut, contained chariots, couches, and a throne—all decorated with gold.

This small gold statue of King Tut was found in his tomb.

Pharaoh Tutankhamen's golden throne

A Mummy for All Time

To live on in the afterlife, the ancient Egyptians believed a person also needed his or her body. Therefore, it was very important that the body be **preserved**. Special workers called **embalmers** covered the body with salt to dry it. Next, they rubbed the shriveled body with oils, animal fat, and beeswax. Then, they made the body into a mummy by wrapping it with bandages.

Before preserving a body, embalmers first removed the liver, lungs, intestines, and stomach.

Amulets

As embalmers wrapped a mummy, they placed small good luck charms called amulets between the bandages. The amulets were thought to ensure that the dead person was safe, healthy, and happy in the afterlife.

Finally, the mummy was laid in a coffin and placed inside a sarcophagus in a tomb. A person's spirit was thought to have a strong connection to its mummified body. It was believed that the spirit would visit the mummy. If the mummy was destroyed or removed from its tomb, the connection would be broken. Then the spirit could not live on in the afterlife and would disappear forever!

Before a dead body was wrapped, it might be decorated with jewelry. This gold bracelet was found on a pharaoh's mummy.

This painting on a sarcophagus shows a spirit (with wings) visiting its mummy.

Grave Goods for Sale

Sometimes a tomb was robbed soon after a person's funeral. Other tombs remained hidden and sealed up for centuries before robbers finally discovered them. When thieves broke into a tomb, they took goods that were easy to carry and sell. Jewelry and other items made of copper, bronze, silver, or gold were highly prized. These could be sold, or they might be melted down and made into new pieces of jewelry, amulets, and other objects.

A gold bracelet

Once it melted, gold cooled and hardened into lumps. Then it could be used to buy goods.

Wooden furniture decorated with gold and ivory was also valuable to thieves. If a burial was recent, robbers stole fresh makeup, perfumed oils, and even clothes that had been buried with the mummy. Theives often used stolen goods to buy food, cattle, or land.

An ancient Egyptian box containing bottles of makeup and perfumed oils

Sometimes robbers sold objects to criminal go-betweens known as fences. A fence is a person who buys stolen goods from a thief and then sells them to a customer—often far from the robbery.

Who Were the Robbers?

Ancient Egyptian tomb robbers came from all levels of **society**. Some were poorly paid workers, like Amenpanufer. These thieves turned to a life of crime to bring in extra money for their families. Yet, even important members of society were involved in robbing tombs or buying and selling stolen goods. Old records tell of priests, soldiers, and government officials taking part in the crimes.

This painting shows priests at a funeral preparing a mummy to enter the afterlife. Sometimes priests stole valuable goods from a tomb soon after the mummy was laid inside!

Occasionally, the thieves were even the men who built the pharaohs' tombs! Many kings, queens, and other important Egyptians were buried in a huge cemetery called the Valley of the Kings. Their tombs were dug into the valley's rocky cliffs by tomb builders. Sometimes, as workers built new tombs, they robbed the older tombs. Then they would **smuggle** the treasures out of the valley to sell them.

This picture shows the Valley of the Kings today. In ancient times, the tomb entrances were sealed up and hidden beneath rock and sand.

A special police force called the Medjay guarded the Valley of the Kings. Despite their protection, however, over the centuries thieves were able to raid almost all the tombs in the valley.

The Story of a Thief

Eventually, Amenpanufer's life of crime caught up with him. He was arrested and thrown in jail to await **trial**. How is so much known about his life? In the mid-1800s, 3,000-year-old documents were dug up in the ruins of the ancient city of Thebes. The documents, called **papyri**, contain a detailed record of Amenpanufer's trial.

This section of a papyrus mentions tomb robbing from Amenpanufer's time.

Papyri are made from papyrus plants.

According to the record, Amenpanufer was **interrogated** by officials at Thebes. Every word was recorded by a writer called a scribe. To make Amenpanufer confess to his crimes, his hands and feet were brutally beaten with a stick. Finally, the young thief admitted that he had robbed Pharaoh Sobekemsaf's tomb. Then, he was found guilty and sentenced to death!

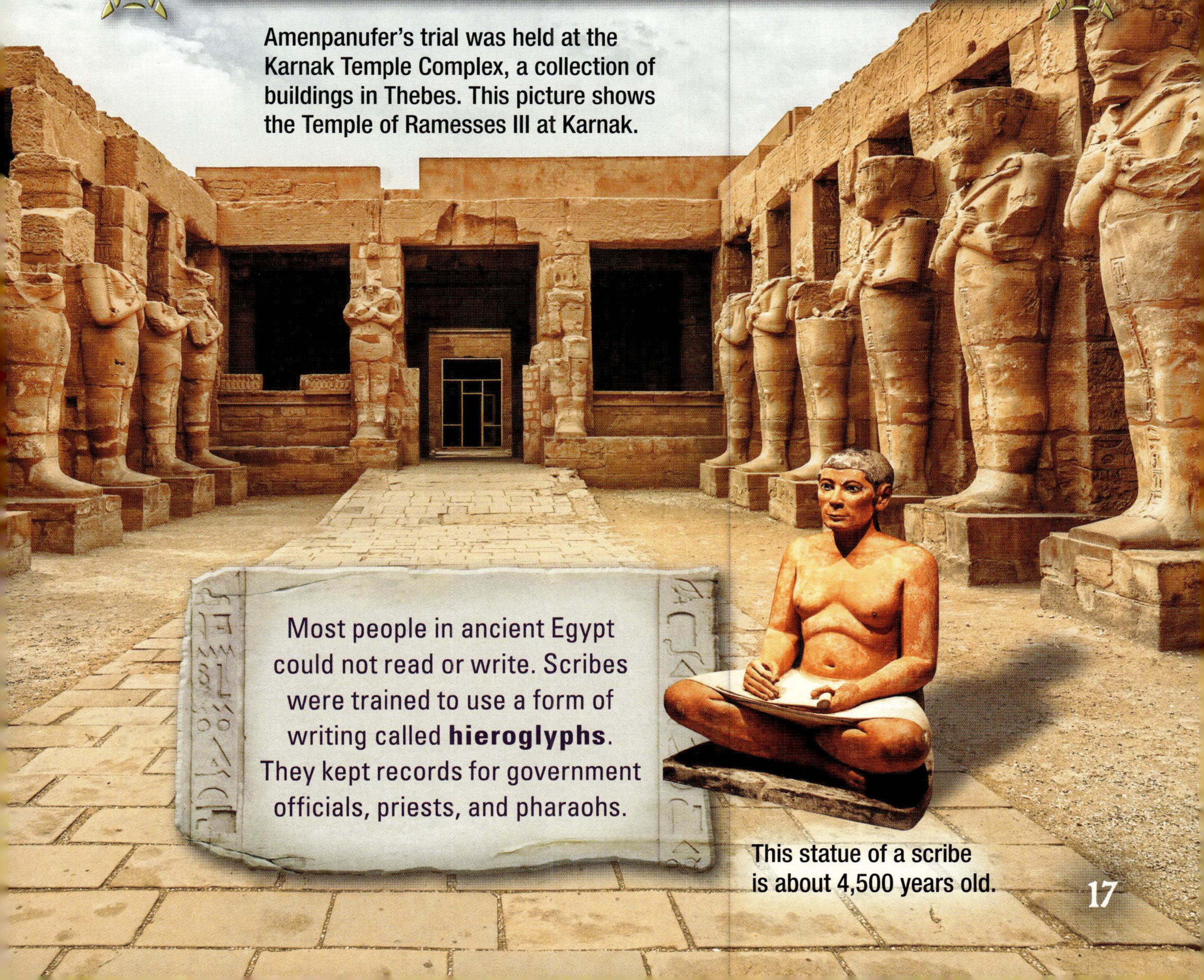

Amenpanufer's trial was held at the Karnak Temple Complex, a collection of buildings in Thebes. This picture shows the Temple of Ramesses III at Karnak.

Most people in ancient Egypt could not read or write. Scribes were trained to use a form of writing called **hieroglyphs**. They kept records for government officials, priests, and pharaohs.

This statue of a scribe is about 4,500 years old.

The Worst Punishment

After Amenpanufer was sentenced, he was probably taken into the desert along with his accomplices. While still alive, each man was **impaled** on a tall spike that was sharpened to a point at the top. If the spike pierced his heart, the man died instantly. If not, he would experience a slow, agonizing death in the hot desert sun.

For the ancient Egyptians, robbing a pharaoh was the worst crime possible. Disturbing a mummy and its tomb were also horrific crimes. For committing these acts, a tomb robber received the most terrible punishment possible. After he died, Amenpanufer's body may have been left to rot in the desert. He would have no mummy or tomb, so he would never reach the afterlife!

How would a tomb robber's death sentence have been recorded by a scribe? The writer would have used this hieroglyph to mean "death by impalement."

Stopping the Thieves

Tomb builders tried many different tricks to prevent theft. The Great Pyramid of Giza, near the city of Cairo, was built as a tomb for Pharaoh Khufu about 4,500 years ago. The builders installed three giant slabs of stone in the ceiling of the passage that led to the burial chamber. The thick, heavy stones were held in place by ropes. Once the Pharaoh's mummy was placed inside the burial chamber, the stones were lowered—completely blocking the passage.

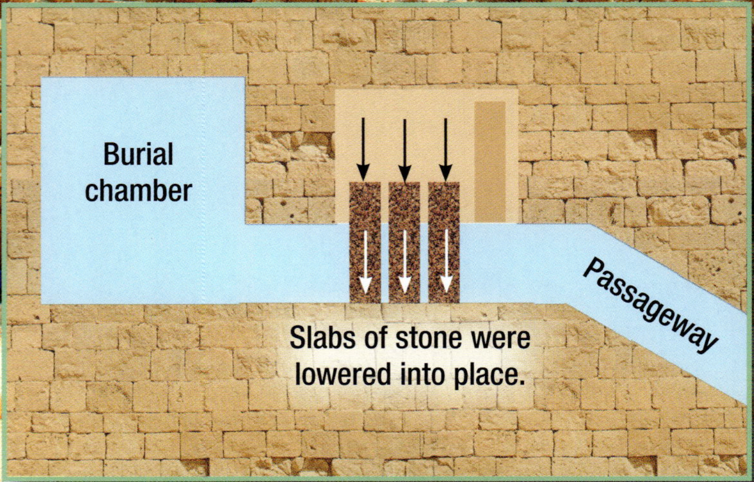

This diagram shows how Khufu's burial chamber was protected.

The entrance to Khufu's tomb was then sealed up with blocks that matched the rest of the pyramid's exterior. From the outside, it was impossible to see where the entrance had been. Today, however, the burial chamber is empty. No one has ever found Khufu's mummy or any treasures in his pyramid. It seems that despite all the tricks, robbers still found a way in!

The entrance to the Great Pyramid would not have been seen when it was covered with blocks.

Sometimes tomb builders created passageways that led to dead ends or empty chambers. The tricks made finding a burial chamber harder for the robbers, but it didn't stop them.

The Hidden Mummies

By the 900s B.C., tomb robbing was **rampant** in the Valley of the Kings. To protect the royal mummies in the valley, priests had no choice but to take more than 40 mummies from their tombs and hide them in a secret location. Alongside the mummies, they also hid around 6,000 valuable items. The mummies' hiding place remained undiscovered . . . for around 2,700 years.

This is the area on the west bank of the Nile River where the mummies were hidden.

Then, one day in the 1870s, a man named Ahmed Abd el-Rassul found the hidden **cache** of mummies. El-Rassul kept the discovery a secret from the world. Then he and his brothers began robbing the tomb. The El-Rassuls sold treasures from the cache as **souvenirs** to wealthy Europeans visiting Egypt. They even sold some of the mummies!

This deep hole is the entrance to the mummies' hiding place.

A man selling mummies on a street in Egypt in the 1800s

El-Rassul found the mummies while searching for his lost goat. The animal had fallen down a hole in a rocky desert area called Deir el-Bahri. While rescuing the goat, El-Rassul made the incredible discovery.

Mixed-Up Mummies

For around ten years, the El-Rassul brothers **plundered** the mummy cache. Then, in 1881, Egyptian government officials learned of the hidden tomb. They rescued the mummies that remained in the cache and took them to a museum in Cairo.

Once **Egyptologists** examined the mummies, they had a huge puzzle to solve. When the anicent priests had moved the bodies, they wrote the mummies' names on documents called dockets and attached these to the bandages. The coffins also had dockets identifying who was inside.

This artwork from the late 1890s shows Egyptologists examining one of the mummies from the cache.

Yet, some of the mummies in the cache had no dockets. Others were in the wrong coffins. This may have happened when the priests rushed to move the mummies to the hiding place. The El-Rassuls probably added to the chaos as they searched inside the coffins, looking for valuable objects. Eventually, the Egyptologists unraveled much of the confusion. However, some of the mummies still have not been identified.

In 1898, the tomb of Pharaoh Amenhotep II was discovered in the Valley of the Kings. Also in the tomb were 17 other mummies that had been hidden away from robbers in ancient times. Once again, there were no clues to identify some of the mummies.

This mummy was found in the second cache, in Amenhotep II's tomb, without a docket. In 2010, Egyptologists carried out tests that proved she is King Tut's grandmother Queen Tiye (TEE-ay).

Then and Now

When Egyptologists studied the mummies from the two caches, many were badly damaged. This happened when ancient thieves robbed the tombs. Some mummies had holes in their skulls, probably made by a tool called an adze. The robbers would often hack at the mummies' bandages to find the amulets and jewelry beneath the wrappings.

An ancient Egyptian carpenter using an adze to build a boat

Under the mummy wrappings of Pharaoh Thutmose (TUTH-moh-say) III, Egyptologists found four pieces of wood. The mummy had been damaged by tomb robbers. However, ancient officials had used the wood as **splints** to keep the mummy's body in position before rewrapping it.

One mummy had her right arm torn off. Her face and chest were also crushed. She is called the "Younger Lady" mummy because her name is not known.

Today, the mummies from the caches are safe in museums around the world. Scientists continue to study the bodies and learn more about them. Yet what became of all the ancient tomb robbers who **desecrated** their tombs? Were they punished in this world . . . or perhaps the next? The question remains . . .

Egyptologists have done tests that show the "Younger Lady" mummy is King Tut's mother.

Egypt's Ancient Secrets

Egyptologist are studying many mysteries left behind by tomb robbers, but the search for answers goes on.

The Fate of Ramesses I

The coffin of Pharaoh Ramesses I was discovered in the Deir el-Bahri tomb. When Egyptologists opened the coffin, however, all they found was a tangle of linen bandages. Where was the king? In the 1800s, the El-Rassul brothers sold the mummy and it eventually ended up in a museum in Canada. The mummy was put on display as a curiosity for almost 130 years. Then, in 1999, the mummy was sold to a museum in Atlanta. At that time, experts identified it as being the famous Egyptian king. In 2003, Ramesses I was finally returned to Egypt.

The mummy of Ramesses I

Are There More Hidden Tombs?

In ancient times, tomb builders did all they could to hide tombs. In the Valley of the Kings, they dug tombs deep beneath the rock and sand. Some experts believe many tombs are so well hidden that they have not yet been discovered. Egyptologists have never found the tombs of Pharaoh Thutmose II, Ramesses VIII, the famous Queen Nefertiti—and many others. If they are found, will they contain ancient treasure?

A bust of Nefertiti

Does the Mummy's Curse Exist?

A scene from the 1964 movie, *The Curse of the Mummy's Tomb*

There have been many stories about mummies putting curses on people who dared to enter their tombs. Could the stories be true? Near the tomb of a priest named Amenhotep, Egyptologists found a curse carved in stone that threatened terrible things to any intruders. The curse said that a person who damaged Amenhotep's tomb would be starved, burned, and drowned! Have any mummy curses actually come true? It's very unlikely. In fact, most stories of curses actually come from old movies, not ancient Egypt.

Glossary

accomplices (uh-KAHM-pliss-uhs) people who help someone do something illegal or wrong

afterlife (AF-tur-*life*) the life a person has after he or she dies

cache (KASH) a hiding place

desecrated (DESS-uh-*kray*-tid) damaged or treated with disrespect, especially objects or places with religious importance

Egyptologists (ee-jip-TAHL-uh-jists) historians or scientists who study ancient Egypt

embalmers (em-BALM-urz) people who prepare dead bodies for burial

hieroglyphs (HYE-ur-uh-*glifss*) pictures used in Egyptian writing

impaled (im-PAYLD) killed by piercing with a sharpened stake or pole

interrogated (in-TERR-uh-*gayt*-id) questioned in an official and sometimes aggressive way, usually about a crime

mummy (MUH-mee) the preserved body of a dead person or animal

papyri (puh-PYE-ree) ancient papers made from the stems of the papyrus plant

pendants (PEN-dunts) ornaments hung from chains and worn around the neck

pharaoh (FAIR-oh) a ruler of ancient Egypt

plundered (PLUN-durd) stole from

preserved (prih-ZURVD) treated something to stop it from rotting

rampant (RAM-puhnt) not checked in growth or spread

sarcophagi (sar-KAHF-uh-gye) large stone boxes made for holding coffins

smuggle (SMUG-uhl) secretly bring goods in or out of a place

society (suh-SYE-uh-tee) all the people who live in the same country or area and share the same laws and customs

souvenirs (soo-vuh-NIHRZ) objects that are purchased as a reminder of a place

spirit (SPIHR-it) the part of a person that may go on after death

splints (SPLINTZ) pieces of wood used to hold a broken bone in place

status (STA-tuhs) how important or high-ranking a person is within their society

stonemason (STOHN-may-suhn) a person who carves statues or builds structures from stone

tomb (TOOM) a grave, room, or building in which a dead body is placed

trial (TRYE-uhl) an examination of evidence in a court to decide if a person is guilty or not guilty of a crime

Bibliography

Reeves, Nicholas, and Richard H. Wilkinson. *The Complete Valley of the Kings: Tombs and Treasures of Egypt's Greatest Pharaohs.* New York: Thames & Hudson (2008).

Romer, John. *The Great Pyramid: Ancient Egypt Revisited.* Cambridge, UK: Cambridge University Press (2007).

Read More

Allen, Kathy. *Ancient Egyptian Hieroglyphs (Fact Finders: Ancient Egyptian Civilization).* North Mankato, MN: Capstone (2016).

Dickmann, Nancy. *Ancient Egypt: Dig up the Secrets of the Dead (History Hunters).* North Mankato, MN: Capstone (2017).

Hart, George. *Ancient Egypt (DK Eyewitness Books).* New York: Dorling Kindersley (2014).

Lunis, Natalie. *Tut's Deadly Tomb (HorrorScapes).* New York: Bearport (2011).

Learn More Online

To learn more about tomb robbers, visit
www.bearportpublishing.com/EgyptsAncientSecrets

Index

afterlife 8–9, 10–11, 14, 19
Amenhotep II, Pharaoh 25
Amenhotep (priest) 29
Amenpanufer 6–7, 14, 16–17, 18–19
amulets 10, 12, 26

Cairo 4, 20, 24
curses 29

desert 4, 18–19, 23

Egyptologists 24–25, 26–27, 28–29
El-Rassul, Ahmed Abd 23, 24–25
El-Rassul brothers 23, 24–25, 28
embalmers 10

gold 6–7, 8–9, 11, 12–13
Great Pyramid 20–21

hieroglyphs 17, 19

jewelry 6–7, 9, 11, 12, 26

Khufu, Pharaoh 20–21

mummies 6–7, 10–11, 14, 19, 20–21, 22–23, 24–25, 26–27, 28–29

Nefertiti, Queen 29
Nile River 4, 22

papyri 16
priests 14, 17, 22, 24–25, 29

Ramesses I, Pharaoh 28
Ramesses III, Pharaoh 17
Ramesses VI, Pharaoh 15
Ramesses VIII, Pharaoh 29

sarcophagi 6–7, 11
scribes 17, 19
Sobekemsaf, Pharaoh 4–5, 7, 17

Thebes 4, 16–17
Thutmose II, Pharaoh 29
Thutmose III, Pharaoh 26
Tiye, Queen 25
tombs 4–5, 6–7, 8–9, 11, 12, 14–15, 16–17, 19, 20–21, 22–23, 24–25, 26–27, 28–29
Tutankhamen, Pharaoh 9, 15, 25

Valley of the Kings 4, 15, 22, 25, 29

About the Author

Ruth Owen has written many nonfiction books for children. She has always been fascinated by ancient Egyptian history and the work of archaeologists.